Spaghetti Recipes

Every Possible

Way

30 Flavors for Pický Eaters

Table of Contents

Introduction

If you are into Italian cuisine, especially pasta, this book will be more than handy. I made sure that I covered every popular flavor and variation on how spaghetti is cooked, so I have included spaghetti in tomato sauce, white sauce, and one pot pasta. I found that one-pot pasta is trendy nowadays.

Firstly, invented by Martha Steward, it has become a staple dinner or lunch dish for many American families. It would help if you put all the necessary ingredients in a pot, bring it to a boil for 10-12 minutes, and the result is creamy and rich pasta for everyone in your family.

Once you make one recipe from this book, I am sure you can't wait to make the other one. Every recipe is tasted to ensure that I provide you with the best spaghetti recipes you will ever find. Happy cooking.

1. Classic Spaghetti with Tomato Sauce

If you are looking for a foolproof spaghetti recipe in tomato sauce, you will want to try this recipe. It's simple, has fresh ingredients, and is so easy to put together.

Servings: 2

Time: 15 minutes

The list of ingredients:

- 1/2 pound spaghetti
- salt and pepper to taste

- 1 ½ cups tomato sauce
- 2 tablespoons olive oil
- 1 garlic clove (minced)
- 2 tablespoons freshly chopped basil

Methods:

A. Boil your spaghetti until al dente or for about 4-5 minutes.
B. In a saucepan over medium heat, warm the olive oil and place in the minced garlic.
C. Pour in the tomato sauce and season with salt and pepper to taste.
D. Drain the spaghetti and stir it into the tomato sauce.
E. Cook for about 2 minutes and serve with a sprinkle of chopped basil.
F. Enjoy.

2. Tuna Spaghetti

Tuna spaghetti is a fantastic dish popular in Italy around its coast. You will love this tomato sauce and tuna pasta recipe that will always be a great lunch or dinner idea.

Servings: 2

Time: 15 minutes

The list of ingredients:

- 1/2 pound spaghetti
- salt and pepper to taste
- 1 ½ cups tomato sauce
- 2 tablespoons olive oil

- 1 garlic clove (minced)
- 7 ounces canned tuna (drained)
- 2 tablespoons freshly chopped basil

Methods:

A. Boil your spaghetti until al dente or for about 4-5 minutes.
B. In a saucepan over medium heat, warm the olive oil and place in the minced garlic.
C. Pour in the tomato sauce and season with salt and pepper to taste. Stir in the drained tuna and mix until combined.
D. Drain the spaghetti and stir it into the tomato sauce.
E. Cook for about 2 minutes and serve with a sprinkle of chopped basil.
F. Enjoy.

3. Parmesan Spaghetti

This is a fantastic dish that is perfect for quick lunch or dinner, and it's even more, tastier shared with family or friends.

Servings: 2

Time: 15 minutes

The list of ingredients:

- 1/2 pound spaghetti
- salt and pepper to taste
- 1 ½ cups tomato sauce

- 2 tablespoons olive oil
- 1 garlic clove (minced)
- 2 ounces grated parmesan cheese
- 2 tablespoons freshly chopped basil

Methods:

A. Boil your spaghetti until al dente or for about 4-5 minutes.
B. In a saucepan over medium heat, warm the olive oil and place in the minced garlic.
C. Pour in the tomato sauce and season with salt and pepper to taste.
D. Drain the spaghetti and stir it into the tomato sauce.
E. Cook for about 2 minutes and serve with a sprinkle of chopped basil. Sprinkle some grated parmesan cheese.
F. Enjoy.

4. Capers Spaghetti

Tomato sauce and capers are perfect with each other. This pasta dish will inspire you to cook pasta more often.

Servings: 2

Time: 15 minutes

The list of ingredients:

- 1/2 pound spaghetti
- salt and pepper to taste
- 1 ½ cups tomato sauce
- 2 tablespoons olive oil

- 1 garlic clove (minced)
- 3 tablespoons capers
- 2 tablespoons freshly chopped basil

Methods:

A. Boil your spaghetti until al dente or for about 4-5 minutes.
B. In a saucepan over medium heat, warm the olive oil and place in the minced garlic.
C. Pour in the tomato sauce and season with salt and pepper to taste.
D. Drain the spaghetti and stir it into the tomato sauce. Stir in the capers.
E. Cook for about 2 minutes and serve with a sprinkle of chopped basil.
F. Enjoy.

5. Shrimp Spaghetti

Shrimp in spaghetti and tomato sauce is perfect. You will make this dish more often once you give this one a try.

Servings: 2

Time: 15 minutes

The list of ingredients:

- 1/2 pound spaghetti
- salt and pepper to taste
- 1 ½ cups tomato sauce
- 2 tablespoons olive oil

- 1 garlic clove (minced)
- 1/2 pound shrimps (cleaned)
- 2 tablespoons freshly chopped basil

Methods:

A. Boil your spaghetti until al dente or for about 4-5 minutes.
B. In a saucepan over medium heat, warm the olive oil and place in the minced garlic.
C. Pour in the tomato sauce and season with salt and pepper to taste. Stir in the shrimps and cook them for about 2-3 minutes.
D. Drain the spaghetti and stir it into the tomato sauce.
E. Cook for about 2 minutes and serve with a sprinkle of chopped basil.
F. Enjoy.

6. Olive Spaghetti

Olives – black and green will work in this recipe. I suggest you use calamata olives because they release the best flavor and taste in this recipe.

Servings: 2

Time: 15 minutes

The list of ingredients:

- 1/2 pound spaghetti
- salt and pepper to taste
- 1 ½ cups tomato sauce

- 2 tablespoons olive oil
- 1 garlic clove (minced)
- 1/4 cup diced calamata olives
- 2 tablespoons freshly chopped basil

Methods:

A. Boil your spaghetti until al dente or for about 4-5 minutes.
B. In a saucepan over medium heat, warm the olive oil and place in the minced garlic.
C. Pour in the tomato sauce and season with salt and pepper to taste. Stir in the diced olives.
D. Drain the spaghetti and stir it into the tomato sauce.
E. Cook for about 2 minutes and serve with a sprinkle of chopped basil.
F. Enjoy.

7. Zucchini Spaghetti

Zucchinis are perfect in pasta recipes. This spaghetti recipe is delicious and full of flavor. You will enjoy every single bite of it, and drizzle just extra virgin olive oil at the end to empower the whole dish even more with flavor.

Servings: 2

Time: 15 minutes

The list of ingredients:

- 1/2 pound spaghetti
- salt and pepper to taste

- 1 ½ cups tomato sauce
- 2 tablespoons olive oil
- 1 garlic clove (minced)
- 1 small zucchini (sliced)
- 2 tablespoons freshly chopped basil

Methods:

A. Boil your spaghetti until al dente or for about 4-5 minutes.
B. In a saucepan over medium heat, warm the olive oil and place in the minced garlic.
C. Stir in the sliced zucchini and stir until the zucchini starts to wilt down a bit.
D. Pour in the tomato sauce and season with salt and pepper to taste.
E. Drain the spaghetti and stir it into the tomato sauce.
F. Cook for about 2 minutes and serve with a sprinkle of chopped basil.
G. Enjoy.

8. Beef Spaghetti

Ground meat in spaghetti brings that Bolognese flavor to every pasta recipe. You will enjoy this tomato sauce with ground beef and chopped basil. It's the best quick sauce you have ever tried.

Servings: 2

Time: 15 minutes

The list of ingredients:

- 1/2 pound spaghetti
- salt and pepper to taste

- 1 ½ cups tomato sauce
- 2 tablespoons olive oil
- 1 garlic clove (minced)
- 1/2 pound ground beef
- 2 tablespoons freshly chopped basil

Methods:

A. Boil your spaghetti until al dente or for about 4-5 minutes.
B. In a saucepan over medium heat, warm the olive oil and place in the minced garlic.
C. Stir in the ground beef and cook for 2-3 minutes until crumbly.
D. Pour in the tomato sauce and season with salt and pepper to taste.
E. Drain the spaghetti and stir it into the tomato sauce.
F. Cook for about 2 minutes and serve with a sprinkle of chopped basil.
G. Enjoy.

9. Red wine tomato sauce Spaghetti

This tomato sauce is not a regular one, and it's infused with red wine to give the best flavor. You will enjoy every bite of this Spaghetti because you will feel the rich flavor of the sauce.

Servings: 2

Time: 15 minutes

The list of ingredients:

- 1/2 pound spaghetti
- salt and pepper to taste

- 1 ½ cups tomato sauce
- 2 tablespoons olive oil
- 1 garlic clove (minced)
- 3 tablespoons red wine
- 2 tablespoons grated parmesan cheese
- 2 tablespoons freshly chopped basil

Methods:

A. Boil your Spaghetti until al dente or for about 4-5 minutes.

B. In a saucepan over medium heat, warm the olive oil and place in the minced garlic.

C. Pour in the tomato sauce and season with salt and pepper to taste. Pour the red wine

D. Drain the Spaghetti and stir it into the tomato sauce.

E. Cook for about 2 minutes and serve with a sprinkle of chopped basil and grated parmesan cheese.

F. Enjoy.

10. Cherry tomato Spaghetti

Imagine your bowl of Spaghetti with little cherry tomatoes and a sprinkle of freshly chopped basil on top.

Servings: 2

Time: 15 minutes

The list of ingredients:

- 1/2 pound spaghetti
- salt and pepper to taste
- 10 ounces cherry tomatoes (diced)
- 2 tablespoons olive oil

- 1 garlic clove (minced)
- 2 tablespoons grated parmesan cheese
- 2 tablespoons freshly chopped basil

Methods:

A. Boil your Spaghetti until al dente or for about 4-5 minutes.
B. In a saucepan over medium heat, warm the olive oil and place in the minced garlic.
C. Stir in the diced cherry tomatoes and season with salt and pepper to taste. Pour the red wine
D. Drain the Spaghetti and stir it into the tomato sauce.
E. Cook for about 2 minutes and serve with a sprinkle of chopped basil and grated parmesan cheese.
F. Enjoy.

11. Alfredo sauce Spaghetti

This white sauce is perfect if you want to try something new and different from tomato sauce. It's richer in flavor and tastier than tomato sauce.

Servings: 2

Time: 15 minutes

The list of ingredients:

- 1/2 pound spaghetti
- salt and pepper to taste
- 2 tablespoons butter

- 1 garlic clove (minced)
- 1 tablespoon flour
- 1 cup heavy cream
- 1/2 cup whole milk
- 2 ounces Grated parmesan cheese

Methods:

A. Boil your Spaghetti until al dente or for about 4-5 minutes.

B. In a saucepan over medium heat, warm the butter and place in the minced garlic.

C. Stir in the flour and cook for about 2 minutes on medium heat.

D. Stir in the heavy cream and whole milk and mix with the help of a wire whisk.

E. Stir constantly and add in the parmesan cheese.

F. Drain the Spaghetti and stir it into the white sauce.

G. Mix everything until very combined and serve to enjoy.

12. Chicken Spaghetti

If you have some leftover chicken, this is the best recipe for Spaghetti to use it. You will enjoy the creamy and delicious white sauce and delicious chicken taste.

Servings: 2

Time: 15 minutes

The list of ingredients:

- 1/2 pound spaghetti
- salt and pepper to taste
- 2 tablespoons butter

- 1 garlic clove (minced)
- 1 tablespoon flour
- 1 cup heavy cream
- 1/2 cup whole milk
- 7 ounces shredded chicken
- 2 ounces Grated parmesan cheese

Methods:

A. Boil your Spaghetti until al dente or for about 4-5 minutes.

B. In a saucepan over medium heat, warm the butter and place in the minced garlic.

C. Stir in the flour and cook for about 2 minutes on medium heat.

D. Stir in the heavy cream and whole milk and mix with the help of a wire whisk.

E. Stir constantly and add in the parmesan cheese. Add the shredded chicken and mix until combined.

F. Drain the Spaghetti and stir it into the white sauce.

G. Mix everything until very combined and serve to enjoy.

13. Cheesy Spaghetti

I love some excellent cheese spaghetti, and this is the recipe you are looking for if you love some cheesy spaghetti. Three types of cheeses are enough for every cheese lover.

Servings: 2

Time: 15 minutes

The list of ingredients:

- 1/2 pound spaghetti
- salt and pepper to taste
- 2 tablespoons butter

- 1 garlic clove (minced)
- 1 tablespoon flour
- 1 cup heavy cream
- 1/2 cup whole milk
- 1/2 cup grated mozzarella cheese
- 1/2 cup grated gouda cheese
- 2 ounces Grated parmesan cheese

Methods:

A. Boil your Spaghetti until al dente or for about 4-5 minutes.

B. In a saucepan over medium heat, warm the butter and place in the minced garlic.

C. Stir in the flour and cook for about 2 minutes on medium heat.

D. Stir in the heavy cream and whole milk and mix with the help of a wire whisk.

E. Stir constantly and add in the parmesan cheese, gouda cheese, and mozzarella cheese.

F. Drain the Spaghetti and stir it into the white sauce.

G. Mix everything until very combined and serve to enjoy.

14. Blue cheese Spaghetti

Blue cheese in your Spaghetti will bring so much flavor. This is a perfect recipe for everyone who loves excellent and classic flavors.

Servings: 2

Time: 15 minutes

The list of ingredients:

- 1/2 pound spaghetti
- salt and pepper to taste
- 2 tablespoons butter

- 1 garlic clove (minced)
- 1 tablespoon flour
- 1 cup heavy cream
- 1/2 cup whole milk
- 2 ounces crumbled blue cheese
- 2 ounces Grated parmesan cheese

Methods:

A. Boil your Spaghetti until al dente or for about 4-5 minutes.

B. In a saucepan over medium heat, warm the butter and place in the minced garlic.

C. Stir in the flour and cook for about 2 minutes on medium heat.

D. Stir in the heavy cream and whole milk and mix with the help of a wire whisk.

E. Stir constantly and add in the parmesan cheese and blue cheese.

F. Drain the Spaghetti and stir it into the white sauce.

G. Mix everything until very combined and serve to enjoy

15. Honey infused Spaghetti

If you love a sweet touch to your pasta dish, then this Spaghetti is perfect for every occasion.

Servings: 2

Time: 15 minutes

The list of ingredients:

- 1/2 pound spaghetti
- salt and pepper to taste
- 2 tablespoons butter
- 1 garlic clove (minced)

- 1 tablespoon flour
- 1 cup heavy cream
- 1/2 cup whole milk
- 1 tablespoon honey
- 2 ounces Grated parmesan cheese

Methods:

A. Boil your Spaghetti until al dente or for about 4-5 minutes.
B. In a saucepan over medium heat, warm the butter and place in the minced garlic.
C. Stir in the flour and cook for about 2 minutes on medium heat.
D. Stir in the heavy cream and whole milk and mix with the help of a wire whisk.
E. Stir constantly and add in the parmesan cheese and honey
F. Drain the Spaghetti and stir it into the white sauce.
G. Mix everything until very combined and serve to enjoy.

16. Shrimp Spaghetti in white sauce

Shrimps are perfect in tomato sauce, but if you want them even tastier, you need to try this white sauce.

Servings: 2

Time: 15 minutes

The list of ingredients:

- 1/2 pound spaghetti
- salt and pepper to taste
- 2 tablespoons butter
- 1 garlic clove (minced)

- 1 tablespoon flour
- 1 cup heavy cream
- 1/2 pound shrimps (cleaned)
- 2 oz. Grated parmesan cheese

Methods:

A. Boil your Spaghetti until al dente or for about 4-5 minutes.
B. In a saucepan over medium heat, warm the butter and place in the minced garlic.
C. Stir in the flour and shrimps and cook them for about 1-2 minutes.
D. Stir in the heavy cream and whole milk and mix with the help of a wire whisk.
E. Stir constantly and add in the parmesan cheese.
F. Drain the Spaghetti and stir it into the white sauce.
G. Mix everything until very combined and serve to enjoy.

17. Lemon spaghetti

Creamy, lemony, and perfect for the summertime, this spaghetti recipe is a decadent and rich meal for everyone.

Servings: 2

Time: 15 minutes

The list of ingredients:

- 1/2 pound spaghetti
- salt and pepper to taste
- 2 tablespoons butter
- 1 garlic clove (minced)

- 1 tablespoon flour
- 1 cup heavy cream
- 1 lemon juice and zest
- 2 ounces Grated parmesan cheese

Methods:

A. Boil your Spaghetti until al dente or for about 4-5 minutes.

B. In a saucepan over medium heat, warm the butter and place in the minced garlic.

C. Stir in the flour and cook them for about 1-2 minutes.

D. Stir in the heavy cream and whole milk and mix with the help of a wire whisk.

E. Stir constantly and add the zest and juice of the lemon and grated parmesan cheese.

F. Drain the Spaghetti and stir it into the white sauce.

G. Mix everything until very combined and serve to enjoy.

18. Garlic butter spaghetti

If you love some excellent garlic flavor in your bowl of Spaghetti, then this is a perfect recipe to try. You will surely enjoy every single bite of it and ask for a second serving.

Servings: 2

Time: 15 minutes

The list of ingredients:

- 1/2 pound spaghetti
- salt and pepper to taste
- 2 tablespoons butter

- 1 garlic clove (minced)
- 1 tablespoon flour
- 1 cup heavy cream
- 3 garlic cloves (minced)
- 1/4 cup chopped parsley
- 2 ounces Grated parmesan cheese

Methods:

A. Boil your Spaghetti until al dente or for about 4-5 minutes.
B. In a saucepan over medium heat, warm the butter and place in the minced garlic.
C. Stir in the flour and minced garlic and cook them for about 1-2 minutes.
D. Stir in the heavy cream and whole milk and mix with the help of a wire whisk.
E. Stir constantly and add chopped parsley and grated parmesan cheese.
F. Drain the Spaghetti and stir it into the white sauce.
G. Mix everything until very combined and serve to enjoy.

19. Peas spaghetti

If you want something green in your white sauce for your Spaghetti, this pea-inspired recipe is a thing to try. You will love the colors on your plate, and the taste will make you crave a second serving.

Servings: 2

Time: 15 minutes

The list of ingredients:

- 1/2 pound spaghetti
- salt and pepper to taste

- 2 tablespoons butter
- 1 tablespoon flour
- 1 cup heavy cream
- 1/2 cup frozen peas
- 2 ounces Grated parmesan cheese

Methods:

A. Boil your Spaghetti until al dente or for about 4-5 minutes.
B. In a saucepan over medium heat, warm the butter and place in the minced garlic.
C. Stir in the flour and cook them for about 1-2 minutes.
D. Stir in the heavy cream and whole milk and mix with the help of a wire whisk.
E. Stir constantly and add frozen peas and grated parmesan cheese.
F. Drain the Spaghetti and stir it into the white sauce.
G. Mix everything until very combined and serve to enjoy.

20. Mushroom spaghetti

This recipe is an absolute favorite in my home. I love mushrooms, and everyone at home loves them too, especially in pasta recipes.

Servings: 2

Time: 15 minutes

The list of ingredients:

- 1/2 pound spaghetti
- salt and pepper to taste
- 2 tablespoons butter

- 1 tablespoon flour
- 1 cup heavy cream
- 7 ounces diced mushrooms
- 2 ounces Grated parmesan cheese

Methods:

A. Boil your Spaghetti until al dente or for about 4-5 minutes.
B. In a saucepan over medium heat, warm the butter and place in the minced garlic.
C. Stir in the flour and diced mushrooms and cook them for about 1-2 minutes.
D. Stir in the heavy cream and whole milk and mix with the help of a wire whisk.
E. Stir constantly and add grated parmesan cheese.
F. Drain the Spaghetti and stir it into the white sauce.
G. Mix everything until very combined and serve to enjoy.

21. One pot spaghetti

One-pot spaghetti recipes are trendy nowadays when you dump everything in a big pot and let them cook for about 15 minutes. This is the classic one-pot recipe that everyone will love.

Servings: 2

Time: 15 minutes

The list of ingredients:

- 1/2 pound spaghetti
- salt and pepper to taste

- 2 tablespoons butter
- 1 garlic clove (minced)
- 1 cup tomato sauce
- 2 cups water
- 1/4 cup chopped parsley
- 3 tablespoons grated parmesan cheese

Methods:

A. To start, place the spaghetti, salt, and pepper in a pot to taste butter, minced garlic clove, tomato sauce, water, and parsley.
B. Bring everything to a boil and cook for about 10-12 minutes or until the liquid is absorbed into the pasta and sauce-like consistency is in the pot.
C. Finally, sprinkle some grated parmesan cheese and serve to enjoy.

22. Tuna one pot spaghetti

If you don't have time to cook two separate pots and pans to make a great pasta dish, then this spaghetti recipe is for you.

Servings: 2

Time: 15 minutes

The list of ingredients:

- 1/2 pound spaghetti
- salt and pepper to taste
- 2 tablespoons butter
- 1 garlic clove (minced)

- 1 cup tomato sauce
- 2 cups water
- 1/4 cup chopped parsley
- 7 ounces canned tuna (drained)
- 3 tablespoons grated parmesan cheese

Methods:

A. To start, place the spaghetti, salt, and pepper in a pot to taste butter, minced garlic clove, tomato sauce, tuna, water, and parsley.
B. Bring everything to a boil and cook for about 10-12 minutes or until the liquid is absorbed into the pasta and sauce-like consistency is in the pot.
C. Finally, sprinkle some grated parmesan cheese and serve to enjoy.

23. Mushroom one pot spaghetti

Mushrooms cooked in this sauce are very juicy and decadent. The ingredients are cooked for about 10 minutes and are all juicy and yummy.

Servings: 2

Time: 15 minutes

The list of ingredients:

- 1/2 pound spaghetti
- salt and pepper to taste
- 2 tablespoons butter

- 1 garlic clove (minced)
- 1 cup tomato sauce
- 2 cups water
- 1/4 cup chopped parsley
- 7 ounces sliced mushrooms
- 3 tablespoons grated parmesan cheese

Methods:

A. To start, place the spaghetti, salt, and pepper in a pot to taste butter, minced garlic clove, tomato sauce, mushrooms, water, and parsley.

B. Bring everything to a boil and cook for about 10-12 minutes or until the liquid is absorbed into the pasta and sauce-like consistency is in the pot.

C. Finally, sprinkle some grated parmesan cheese and serve to enjoy.

24. Capers and onion one pot spaghetti

This dish contains different flavors, and you will enjoy every bite of the creamy and flavorful spaghetti.

Servings: 2

Time: 15 minutes

The list of ingredients:

- 1/2 pound spaghetti
- salt and pepper to taste

- 2 tablespoons butter
- 1 garlic clove (minced)
- 1 cup tomato sauce
- 2 cups water
- 1/4 cup chopped parsley
- 3 tablespoons diced capers
- 1 onion diced
- 3 tablespoons grated parmesan cheese

Methods:

A. To start, place the spaghetti, salt, and pepper in a pot to taste butter, minced garlic clove, tomato sauce, diced onion, diced capers, water, and parsley.

B. Bring everything to a boil and cook for about 10-12 minutes or until the liquid is absorbed into the pasta and sauce-like consistency is in the pot.

C. Finally, sprinkle some grated parmesan cheese and serve to enjoy.

25. Ground beef one pot spaghetti

Ground meat will take only 10 minutes to cook. The flavor that it will release during the cooking time is gorgeous.

Servings: 2

Time: 15 minutes

The list of ingredients:

- 1/2 pound spaghetti
- salt and pepper to taste
- 2 tablespoons butter
- 1 garlic clove (minced)

- 1 cup tomato sauce
- 2 cups water
- 1/4 cup chopped parsley
- 1/2 pound ground beef
- 3 tablespoons grated parmesan cheese

Methods:

A. To start, place the spaghetti, salt, and pepper in a pot to taste butter, minced garlic clove, tomato sauce, ground beef, water, and parsley.
B. Bring everything to a boil and cook for about 10-12 minutes or until the liquid is absorbed into the pasta and sauce-like consistency is in the pot.
C. Finally, sprinkle some grated parmesan cheese and serve to enjoy.

26. Zucchini one pot spaghetti

Creamy, gorgeous, and perfectly seasoned, this zucchini one-pot spaghetti is so good that even the pickiest eaters crave another serving.

Servings: 2

Time: 15 minutes

The list of ingredients:

- 1/2 pound spaghetti
- salt and pepper to taste
- 2 tablespoons butter

- 1 garlic clove (minced)
- 1 cup tomato sauce
- 2 cups water
- 1/4 cup chopped parsley
- 1 zucchini (sliced)
- 3 tablespoons grated parmesan cheese

Methods:

A. To start, place the spaghetti, salt, and pepper in a pot to taste butter, minced garlic clove, tomato sauce, sliced zucchini, water, and parsley.

B. Bring everything to a boil and cook for about 10-12 minutes or until the liquid is absorbed into the pasta and sauce-like consistency is in the pot.

C. Finally, sprinkle some grated parmesan cheese and serve to enjoy.

27. Eggplant one pot spaghetti

Inspired by summer, this spaghetti recipe is terrific. Diced eggplants are used in this recipe, and the flavor is fantastic.

Servings: 2

Time: 15 minutes

The list of ingredients:

- 1/2 pound spaghetti
- salt and pepper to taste
- 2 tablespoons butter
- 1 garlic clove (minced)

- 1 cup tomato sauce
- 2 cups water
- 1/4 cup chopped parsley
- 1 eggplant (diced)
- 3 tablespoons grated parmesan cheese

Methods:

A. To start, place the spaghetti, salt, and pepper in a pot to taste butter, minced garlic clove, tomato sauce, diced eggplant, water, and parsley.

B. Bring everything to a boil and cook for about 10-12 minutes or until the liquid is absorbed into the pasta and sauce-like consistency is in the pot.

C. Finally, sprinkle some grated parmesan cheese and serve to enjoy.

28. Shrimp one pot spaghetti

Even though shrimps require little cooking time, in this one-pot recipe, shrimps are added just 3-4 minutes before the cooking time ends. You will love and enjoy every bite of this dish.

Servings: 2

Time: 15 minutes

The list of ingredients:

- 1/2 pound spaghetti
- salt and pepper to taste

- 2 tablespoons butter
- 1 garlic clove (minced)
- 1 cup tomato sauce
- 2 cups water
- 1/4 cup chopped parsley
- 1/2 pound shrimps (cleaned)
- 3 tablespoons grated parmesan cheese

Methods:

A. To start, place the spaghetti, salt, and pepper in a pot to taste butter, minced garlic clove, tomato sauce, water, and parsley.

B. Bring everything to a boil and cook for about 10-12 minutes or until the liquid is absorbed into the pasta and sauce-like consistency is in the pot.

C. Just 3-4 minutes before the cooking time expires, stir in the cleaned shrimps and cook until everything is creamy and delicious.

D. Finally, sprinkle some grated parmesan cheese and serve to enjoy.

29. Olive one-pot spaghetti

Diced olives are the perfect infusion to this pasta dish. It's creamy and delicious and fantastic to taste. You will enjoy every bite of it, and I am sure about that.

Servings: 2

Time: 15 minutes

The list of ingredients:

- 1/2 pound spaghetti
- salt and pepper to taste
- 2 tablespoons butter

- 1 garlic clove (minced)
- 1 cup tomato sauce
- 2 cups water
- 1/4 cup chopped parsley
- 1/2 cup chopped olives
- 3 tablespoons grated parmesan cheese

Methods:

A. To start, place the spaghetti, salt, and pepper in a pot to taste butter, minced garlic clove, tomato sauce, chopped olives, water, and parsley.

B. Bring everything to a boil and cook for about 10-12 minutes or until the liquid is absorbed into the pasta and sauce-like consistency is in the pot.

C. Finally, sprinkle some grated parmesan cheese and serve to enjoy.

30. Pepper one-pot spaghetti

You will love this next pasta dish if you love tomato sauce and peppers. It's creamy and delicious and everything you need for a summer lunch.

Servings: 2

Time: 15 minutes

The list of ingredients:

- 1/2 pound spaghetti
- salt and pepper to taste
- 2 tablespoons butter

- 1 garlic clove (minced)
- 1 cup tomato sauce
- 2 cups water
- 1/4 cup chopped parsley
- 3 peppers (diced)
- 3 tablespoons grated parmesan cheese

Methods:

A. To start, place the spaghetti, salt, and pepper in a pot to taste butter, minced garlic clove, tomato sauce, diced peppers, water, and parsley.

B. Bring everything to a boil and cook for about 10-12 minutes or until the liquid is absorbed into the pasta and sauce-like consistency is in the pot.

C. Finally, sprinkle some grated parmesan cheese and serve to enjoy.